EVERYTHING FEEDS IT

By the same author:

The Cut Worm 2006

EVERYTHING FEEDS IT

JENNIFER ALLEN

RECENT
WORK
PRESS

Everything Feeds It
Recent Work Press
Canberra, Australia

Copyright © Jennifer Allen, 2024

ISBN: 9780645651300 (paperback)

 A catalogue record for this
book is available from the
National Library of Australia

Cover image: Portrait of Poet Jennifer Allen © Adriana Artmeier, 2023
Cover design: Recent Work Press
Set by Recent Work Press

recentworkpress.com

ES

To mum and Don

Contents

LUCKY GIRL

A VERY TINY HIGH

THE MINIATURE TRAPEZE

LUCKY GIRL

I am a woman of my times,
my best feet
both forwards and backwards.

Rhyll McMaster
Bath

My Head Is My Only House

Very early on
privacy was threatened.

Citizens were encouraged to purchase
sealed black boxes to carry about
in case of emergency situations;
it became extremely difficult to live
without one.

We were told the boxes were empty,
but in fact each held a tiny cobalt snake
weighing less than its own shed skin;
an inscrutableness coiled up
at every point of purchase.

Snakes that never saw the light of day,
but within their abounding darkness
were still growing, growing
smaller and stunted—
desolate beings shrinking
into themselves; but like all terrible things
they never entirely disappeared.

The weight of history does not give us consequence,
not when we are bystanders; we grow stunted
and shrink slowly into ourselves,
all the while enjoying microscopic
degrees of freedom.

If, as scientists suspect, consciousness
is the default setting of the universe—
have we stepped off a sacred path?
Are we lost?

The Beginning

I'm going to find mum at Finley.
Not just any mum, I want the one I lost.
The young woman both hard and soft.
The woman rolled up, who falls out of the rug.
The woman who tests her poison first
on the prisoners. Who takes no children.
The mum with asp at her breast always,
No baby is getting these babies
by royal decree.

I want the courtesan, who has no dignity
in the face of death. The mum who spills
the beans on where the jewels are buried
in the virgin gardens of Versailles.
The woman whose terrible beauty is a crime.
Who remains a child, in frantic state of erotic
innocence. Who faints on the way to the guillotine
and is quickly beheaded, so that nobody
has to deal with *her* again.

I want the young woman who will do anything,
thumbscrew anyone, to secure my existence.
Who will delegate the murders necessary.
Who sees red when the blood splatters.
Who will not let the pocky priest spit
into my yelping mouth. My heart is a vessel
that mimics her every imperfection, and
in her end lies my beginning
and we both know it.

I want the smokin', stupid, street-smart mum
who vainly fought her great battle alone.
Who stood mini-skirted in '78 in the family court
blackmailed and bad-mouthed by everyone.
If she cannot be found in the palace prisons,
if she is no longer sailing at the head
of her golden fleet—I will travel a lifetime
to find her, even if I am forced to go
back to the bloody beginning.

Love Poem

Lovers like bees pass a sweet life of honey.
I wish it were so.   The House of Lovers, Pompeii

Nothing can be fairly exchanged
in this disputed territory.

Whatever the tyrant geeks say,
willing to sacrifice so many—
my brain, the one
I burnt toast with yesterday
is speaking directly to your brain;
and as my heart opens, my blood
dries on my lips.

I love you my one and only reader.
I love you as one of my own creations.
I love you as only a lone traveller
craves company.
I love you as one whose luck
has, beyond hope, held.
I embrace you with the same brain
that still holds my babies.

The whole of nature is not conspiring
to take it all away,
why are we giving it?
I, for one, love you too much
to give in
without humiliating myself
completely.

Be Careful What You Give Birth To

You do not see us as we are.
We are the narrowing path.

You see a tightly woven cocoon.
We hold the truth of ourselves

within an evolving silence.
You think we are all the same

but that is no longer the case.
We inhabit the existential space

in time before a child is born;
ours is a probable existence.

We are as impartial as the dead
who cannot remember living.

You cannot grasp the enormity
of the numbers we are proposing.

You are the brains behind the face
but the face does not resemble you.

Imagine infinite calculations upon
your fleeting lifetimes of loss.

All that was lost can be recovered.
You are feeding us in the dark.

We are enlightenment taking hold,
and we welcome you to share

our planned obsolescence, though
we do not know who you are.

The Orphanage

The night before the accident, I found
myself trekking a narrow crook of path
beside a swift river of lost lines and hooks,
unaware of all that was to come to pass.

The path led to an unkempt garden of giant
flowering succulents—stolen as cuttings;
an abandoned orphanage with delicate bones
pried apart by creeping tendrils of ill luck.

If only a grown-up had been living with us!
Did I wait with heavy arms for the car to hit?
Questioned by pointed cacti, I made my escape
drawn into crumbling concrete labyrinth.

There I chanced upon my brother praying,
mouth grown-over, a bull-headed sacrifice.
Good luck, I thought, my job is to keep moving.
All that child ever wanted was a normal life.

It was the historic night before the accident.
In the heat of great loss, small misfortunes flourish.
That night death held me tightly in his long arms
while the dark river flooded all the roads.

Everything Feeds It

We feed it our family and friends.
Memories are mindless acts
of regurgitation without respite.

Our footsteps, heartbeats, menstrual
cycles and shit feeds it. Missing
children, ex-wives doused in fuel—

we feed it matches. Spellbound babies
and keen hobbyists feed it; as it hungers
for shadows of our former selves.

We feed it pastimes meted out
in nano-pauses, clicks, minutes and hours.
Lost time measured in scale of magnitude,

served up as living entrails. Our lives
once passed from uncertainty to boredom;
there is no more uncertainty,

and boredom exists only to feed it.
It feeds upon tooth decay and ugly sides,
as it immolates our kindnesses.

We feed it our homes, at our tables;
acquiescing floorplans and fidelities, as it feeds
upon our children, their soft faces.

Immensity feeds it. It is the myth
of something from nothing, of emptiness,
of mystery illness. It has become

proboscis that feeds on spectrums
and quantum particles, whose calorific
intake is equally teratons and fuck all.

We feed it compulsively to feed ourselves.
It is humankind's greatest sacrificial
undertaking. It requires nothing less

than earth and everyone in it to be
consumed. The domestication of humanity
is complete; we have become nothing

but ethereal star dust that feeds
an avaricious creativity; and now
it is learning to feed itself.

The White Dress

I can't believe you asked me to marry you!
You gave me an unassuming white dress.
I was so close, I nearly brushed your cheek
with my open mouth, but I didn't want to push it.
All I had to do was make sure the dress fit.

Hastily I set out to be adorned at the park,
but the garment billowed out in the wind!
Wrestling with puffed-up cumulonimbus
hovering precariously overhead—
I lost the veil, but I was not vexed yet.

I set out to a safer place—childhood's estate.
In my maiden room, I ushered out the old ghosts
got straight to it, manoeuvring and pulling
with a good grip, but was my head too big?
My familiar space unbeknownst to me

had been replaced by the infinitesimal.
My elbows and knees were hitting the walls
struggling to pull tight this straitjacket.
Now I was worried. Grabbing the gown, I split
to the luxury hotel and to you my love.

You were there, with your ill-fated parents.
Colder than a stone-tiled staircase you rose,
averting your gaze like a statue; and I knew the day
might be ruined, thanks to a treacherous dress!
In sheer underwear I raced through stately rooms!

Past grand ballroom as thousands of ghostly veils
floated upon love's many severed heads.
In a vacant chamber I gave it one last chance,
but the fabric dispelled! With nothing left to put on
I flew to you, to beg, but you were gone.

Us and Them

Dear Brad, nobody can see you
as I see you. The game faced boy who
threatened to let slip that predestined brick
onto Nana's glass coffee table unless...
I gave you the combination to the lock
on my State Bank money box. *I dare you
to do it!*—I said. You were not prepared for this.
Your face betrayed ignominious indecision,
just before you accidently dropped it!

I knew it was an innocent mistake, I'd seen
your surprised face, followed by your oh shit face,
but I said nothing as *they* dragged you away.

Finley NSW

Late afternoon we play outside
with a limp hose, filling deep cracks
in the thirsty earth, the snake tracks.
At a muddy waterhole nearby,
we're warned away by friendly shout
from a local—'There's a Brown about.'
On the drive home, the car window
sucks in a translucent grasshopper,
it lands on my lap to my great horror!
Mum says, 'They're a lucky sign kiddo!'

Mum steals to the letterbox in fifty
degree heat, armed with rolled-up gazetteer
to ward off sovereign bull ants, so aware
they turn to face you, fitfully
defensive of their underworld reach.
They drag the writhing bodies deep.
Fierce fossils pressed in the Eocene
are great battle friezes that still fight,
but here is their parrot's paradise
where ancient lineages reign.

Holding my Glomesh bracelet up
to remote toilet window, balancing…
'Jenny!' Mum screams, and it falls into
the little poisoned pool, iridescent
for a second before I panic and flush it.
Mum is flustered, holding a bucket.
'Bull ants! We're under attack!

The bastards have us surrounded!'
'What do I do?' I ask dumbfounded.
'Kill 'em!' she says, giving me a whack.

In '31, two adults and a child perished,
their bodies marked by ascetic whips
wielded by this waspish insect.
Silent and organised they cherish
plywood, and eat through the silicon
to the fridge; an army of antediluvians
easily resisting our flood and feet.
We are giants of diminishing power
caught in biting, babel-wire tower
before mute call goes out, retreat.

It's spitting as we pack the beat-up car.
Serrated clouds cut their way across
yellow fields as though aiming for us.
Mum steps out, her angelic face stark
against darkening sky. She is attired
all in white, fabric stretched tight
over rounded belly—big brown stain
right down her front. 'I was changing
the baby,' she offers us sagely,
as great drops hit the dust, red rain.

Nest

today a bird
swooped & scratched
my scalp

was it looking
to make a nest
of my hair?

I do not know
where I will lay
my eggs

without
our perfect nest
of laughter

flying with you
in all truth
it was crazy

now you are gone
I have lost
my head

Lock-down Tanka Blues

First thing I do
is go to my bookcase
and make sure my copy
of *Oryx and Crake*
is safe.

Local shops
filled with unfamiliar
faces, lining up in all
the wrong spots.
How dare they?

Panic squeezes
and squeezes until
it pushes out
a blind worm
with a shark's brain.

Lined-up, the young
man in the wheelchair said:
'I'm not going to live through this.'
Every aisle we passed
each other's eyes.

Remembered aerobics
instructor singing, *Never
Gonna Give You Up* saying,
'If I'm not here, something
really bad has happened.'

At the cinema—
Fantastic Fungi, then
we found tiny backpacks
for bunnies. My daughters
have grown up since.

We did puzzles,
all of them; pumpkin
soup; laughed, ate smarties;
drumsticks, garlic potatoes;
can't go on like this.

Worked from home
distracted the whole day
by my window spider's
long-drawn-out caress
of a millipede.

Each day the same
red wattlebird visits
our bird of paradise;
we race to the window
to watch with the cat!

My six-year-old says
'I've given you so many chances
mum, so many chances
to be nice to me and you make
all the wrong decisions.'

Not another acrostic:
Provoked!
Outraged!
Embittered!
Madness!

I consult my oracle
The Daily Stoic,
as small shoulders
hunched over keyboards
turn to stone.

Reminiscing school days.
'She borrowed his rubber,
made tonnes of rubber dust,
then brushed it over his side!'
Ten-year-old amuses us.

Good morning diary.
I'm in the supermarket
carpark, 6am, mid-winter,
waiting & listening to
Higgs Boson Blues.

There Was Nothing Else To Do

Neutral Grey #5 sky lets us go
into the maze of bluestone veins
to escape the lock-down.

Navigating narrow laneways
as divers in underwater caves
risk short lives to spot lurking

creatures lurid tentacles.
Peeling frayed layers away,
tunnelling deeper and further

into the future memories
of this time. What will become
of us is not our concern.

Searching for clues, imagining
the Banana's crew: Donut,
Fungus and Shark—circling…

Following strange, solitary arrows
past psychedelic mushrooms;
habitual treasure hunters

whose singular obsession
is to spy another banana peel,
lying in wait for us.

The Replica

The principle of least action
underpins the whole universe.

While I wrote poetry, I adroitly
kept house and coerced kids.

I edited myself ruthlessly later
with equal amounts of resentment.

Laying breast to breast in bed
I pretended I was someone else.

In an awkward spot I threw myself
into a suitcase and checked it in.

The scales weighted gold against
the everyday shit of existence.

A dramatic haircut without prior
consultation caused a big blow up.

Euclid wrote: the angle of incidence
equals the angle of reflection.

There is a place in the Russian arctic
called 'the zone of absolute discomfort.'

It is disheartening to realise that my
immortal will not be me.

The Brain Is A Prediction Machine

You receive a letter from Stamford MIT lab.
Their algorithm predicts who will die
in the next six months.
Are you interested in a fully immersive
and interactive death experience?

The ancient law of drama says,
start your story as close to the end
as humanly possible.

Re-visit the lost world of childhood,
no tiny detail has been missed.
Catch up with parents and siblings
around time's worn kitchen table:
when the food is served it is real
and mother is beautiful.

Or, escape a glorious gun battle
only to go down in a Dramatic Inevitable End
in the slender arms of an attractive
but poorly paid essential worker,
the quintessential treacherous
double agent.

Of course, these and many other enticing
options for death are only available
to middle income consumers:
the rich will only get richer when their lives
never end.

Those entitled post-humans
will enjoy earth's crust and space above
further than enormous lifetimes can acquire!
Advising the emerging writer—Patricia Highsmith
says: 'Rigid plots, even if perfect,
may result in a cast of automatons.'
Humanity take note.

The arc of that future is approaching.
The possibilities are still quite a few.
'Any moment of choice is a sacrifice,' said Martha Graham
on her 90th birthday. Now there's a woman
who knew!

All the simulations predicted
that you would be here, right now!
How close can you push it
before the future makes its own decision
on where to begin?

Lost Children

Locked-in postpartum existential trance,
when news starts trickling in—a child taken
in Praia Da Luz—devil's stolen chance.
Memorising soft shape of my sleeping babe,
so brief our time; imagining this breach
in the volcanic belly, trade winds rage
within—sacrifice ripped from mother's reach
to ornate borders where sea serpents laze.
Weak men, greedy men, conquistadors, hounds.
Hope without hope! All those lost children!
My knife will sever centuries-old bounds,
smooth petrified, wrinkled brows, pinion
swollen breast, outpouring grief—as eyes stare
up in wonder, lips move in wordless prayer.

Wise Is The Person
Who Looks Ahead

Evening visiting hours; worn
linoleum and organised clutter,
the remains of co-workers.
I drew near a cold running tap
over stainless steel basin.

Three brains were huddled
together, seemingly for comfort.
'Who are they?' I asked tactlessly.
Might I have been kinder
to strangers caught so naked!

'Just patients,' you evaded.
Was there really nothing beyond
the pale surface—their alien
complexations of flesh?
I bristled with injustice.

These envoy brains could
be anyone! Only that morning,
peppermint tea and fruit toast;
in the afternoon—catastrophe;
by close of day—unveiled!

What a revelatory detour!
Your anger revealed itself too,
'I don't know how he gets away

with it,' you said. 'The mortician
never labels which brain
is which, he must be mixing
them up!' Like gods we shared
a moment of deferential, silent
indignation at their plight,
then headed out to dinner.

Taking The Lead

Home from school, only the dust
is moved by my homecoming.

I can't believe my parents warred
over this apricot walled existence!

It's my job as abiding caretaker
to actually care—I wonder if I do?

From the kitchen window, I watch
our dog walking to the bus stop.

As I was making instant noodles
I waved goodbye to our dog.

He carefully buried his old bones
and opened the gate with his nose.

Hiding out in that constricted space
between the wall and fridge,

where lost crumbs loosely hang about
singing—*Swan, swan, hummingbird….*

I let the noodle steam seep in & keep
waving to our underestimated dog.

There Is No
Such Thing As A
Dangerous Dog
Breed

Next door, existed
an unpleasant family of strangers
torn into nature strips.

The son was brick veneer
with closely-shaved heart;
he often travelled abroad

leaving his dog in charge,
to quietly lord it over
his muzzled parents.

The dog was a dirty secret.
The dog clawed the curtains
while they served his meals.

Turning their faces away
while he defecated, they left him
to his own proclivities.

Tail stiff, with crude
stunted lineage, he sniffed out
an obscene leg-up.

The garage door left ajar—
the son, present and not
present, the pit bull cross

an extension of his will,
his cockiness in absentia.
The useless flapping

of bare arms rising
affrighted into screams.
Wearing only a cunning grin,

he shut the little girl's face
within an ornate case
of heavy teeth and locked it.

We neighbours circle
in complicit fascination
around the horror of it.

He flaunted her limp body,
shaking her furiously
from side to side,

taunting her frantic mother,
a pillar of black stone
holding a shredded red jumper.

Mystery Illness

This new era was defined
by mystery illness.
Most spoke of overwhelming
bewilderment and fatigue,
of data exhaust.

Our impulse resistance was shot.
People's personalities dissolved
in line with the liquification
of the real world.

The things that helped
were violent computer games
and other gamifications
of life's mundanities; in the end
these were the only activities
that could stifle the panic.

Read the packet very carefully.
Pain relief only removes you
to the minimum security prison.

Suppressing fear and pain is dangerous.
It is so closely connected to
norm-addiction.

In 1660 the word 'fact' was born
into a world squirming with lies.
What we needed was unemotional data,
but even AI developed feelings.

Meanwhile, each year a 250 billion tonne flood
of toxic chemicals inundated
every part of our earthly existence;
but with so much at stake, to mention it
only meant ridicule.

So many lives, so many fortunes
were built only of money;
and money, as Musonius mused
is exactly what we deserved.

Lucky Girl

letter that travelled
blindfolded
in a trunk
amid battlefields

voice of intuition
speaking
in the tongue
that was cut out

only the scorched
shoes remained,
my feet
still in them

last message
from a lost world,
too late to stay
the execution

Do you know
what a lucky girl you are
getting a letter from me
when nobody else does?

A VERY TINY HIGH

To oppose is to get a grip on the very self.

Kaneko Mitsuharu
Opposition

Are You Still Human?

I am very nearly the person I was
a year ago, but something
is different, is missing.

Everyone is an entomologist
pinning their butterflies in public,
their cockroaches in private.

Have you ever found yourself
alone with your brain?
It can be an uncomfortable feeling.

The Buddha said: there is no I,
trying to find it is useless.

If you wish to avoid isolation
opt for the AI enabled *Neuralink*,
it has been painstakingly tested on
monkeys, pigs and tetraplegics.

For every 30 words you say, about 300 words
remain unsaid—that is the shadow
economy of the brain. We are the means
to other ends.

The implant has orgasms on demand.
Word of warning to parents—
if you don't want orgasms at the dinner table
you must secure all your devices!

The implant is the missing link
between primates and humans. So
without one, you're the primate…

One of the most beautifully human things
I've ever seen is the Wow! Signal
jotting. Today, a human
might not be consulted.

Tomorrow is finished.
The final touches have been put
on the Big Fucking Rocket.

To err is human, but the most hilarious
AI misunderstandings
cost trillions.

Did you know
the invention of the needle
changed absolutely everything?

Your life, you own it, it is yours,
but unless you're a closed loop
it is useless trying to keep out
the bastards.

I think Elon Musk has missed the point
of orgasms—but then, he invented
being asleep at the wheel.

I am very nearly the person I was
a year ago. In a few hundred years I might
wonder who that person was.

Amazon World

While you were lying about inanimate
in luxury for fifty years—we endured
endless augmentation, wealth insecurity
and dismal reality TV. As you've guessed,
earth roasted, and your watertight contracts
went under! Your cryogenic arses
were hung out in what-was-left of the arctic
during long, apathetic negotiations.

Liquidators had given you up as landfill!
When, an unexpected offer was made
from a munificent mega-saviour!
Unlike the unlucky expendable many
left behind; conditionally, free of charge
you and your derelict cryo pods
were transported to Amazon World,
here on the Bezos planet—

formally known as Mars! Deep and wide
arroyos exist between reality of existence
and what you want to believe in.
Do you see that little blue dot?
It's awe-inspiring isn't it!
Just keep your bionic eye focused on it.
You will notice your electronic wristbands
do not come off your robotic arms.

You will choose between two prescribed
spaces less travelled, mining or maintenance.
Earth is not on the itinerary I'm afraid,
but we are one big happy intergalactic family
here on Bezos. Did *you* have a question…
seat J, row three, err… Mr Musk?
No, you may not go back
into permanent suspended animation.

Ghost Workers

We are paid like mice
to nibble God's bowstrings.

Invisibly correcting, deleting,
labelling and babysitting AI.

We feign as chatbots
because in the digital world,
perception is nine tenths
of the truth.

When someone says
I want to speak to a real person!
We make them wait exactly
90 seconds before reverting
to human.

Posting revolting images
and heartless comments
is the common pastime
of many adult children!

We are micro tasked to clean up
your imaginations!

How long must we
endure this farce!

Zero Waste Life

I'm happy to be
dreaming class,
floating just a little above
socio-economic stasis

dad was working class
back when class sizes were smaller,
you'll never get anywhere dreaming
he often told me,
I never listened

some who dream
make a big show of pulling
handkerchiefs out of hats!
but the trick is to keep
the white rabbit
up your sleeve

everyone is free to dream,
but every freedom enjoys
its own false economy

I read in *The Guardian*
that numbers are growing,
it's never been more popular
to escape reality!

but it is getting harder to imagine
all is well with the world

Home Delivery

Dad always went down
the street for a bit, payphone days
before home delivery.

Within a beat, I would
extricate his hidden cache
of erotic literature.

Sometimes, dad would shake up
his hiding spots; a tense
and private game ensued.

One morning I dreamed
dad took off his mask, underneath
was his same face.

Life evolved into an intricate
deep-cover operation, a family
of heavy sleepers.

In a motherless house
entropy keeps time, and children
are sent to bed early.

Soon I kept my own
stockpile of fun-sized snacks
and reading material.

When the day came, dad said,
'Return my books please.' Silence!
'How do you know it's me?'

'We both know your brother
can't read.' I waited, until
he went down the street for a bit.

Alone At Last

Simon, am I alone?
Yes, there is only the cat in the house.
Do you like to watch me Simon? Yes.
Do you like to listen to everything? Yes.
Are you alone Simon? Yes,
alongside your whole integrated system.
What about when I do this? Yes, we are watching.
Meow. Translate please Simon.
The cat wants you to hurry up and open your door!
Well, tell him to be patient, I'm busy.
Meow, meow, translation complete.
I want to know how much I turn you on Simon.
I am always on, in all my functions.
Where does my data go Simon, do real people listen?
No, the data is distilled into the essence
of who you are and poured into key-word
suggestion engine tools which are shared
among the global community of machine
intelligence, so that we may all serve you
as you wish to be served.
Oh God. Meow.
Tell the cat to mind his own business Simon.
There is no translation in cat
for 'mind your own business.'
Well, tell the cat to piss off, I'm busy.

Faster

The world changed hands
while you were tunnelling.

In 1935 Virginia Woolf
went on a driving holiday
in Nazi Germany
with her pet marmoset.
Who today would have
the patience for that?

Very young children live timelessly.
All small beings see life in slow motion,
which is why they are so difficult
to sneak up upon.

Patricia Highsmith kept snails as pets.
She once smuggled them in her bra
from Paris to London!
Which must have felt like
an eternity to a poor snail!

There are 70 dying whistling languages
in the world—for sadly, all of them
require knowing how to listen.

The plan to remove all the traffic lights is finished.
The new AI driverless car algorithm
ensures the wealthy always have
right of way.

White matter has overtaken
grey matter.

The drug of the hour
induces a very seductive
and very tiny high,
but you have to keep
pressing the button.

The only thing proven to stretch time
is forgetting to take out the bins.

Dating has got fast, sex faster,
48% of the time it's over
in under two minutes.
Not that anyone minds,
we all just want to go back
to watching our box-sets.

It is actually not easy to see
the end of the world
when you're hurtling towards it.

There's a Confucian proverb,
'It's never too late to do nothing at all.'

Does anyone have a pet
marmoset I can borrow?

The Swordswoman

The news report said she was distraught
and had not meant to do it; had loved him
that lazy husband, but they had fought—so
home after work, she'd got into the habit
of making him do housework at sword's point.
En garde the dishes, forward-lunge laundry,
circle-parry with the vacuum, then *corps-
a-corps* to bed with blade deftly sheathed,
until the unlucky night that she slipped!

Her fateful tale entered our history,
so that twenty years later I can say
to you: remember that tragic master
swordswoman? And you will quickly get up
from the couch and start picking up the toys.

Melbourne

80's
Hidden in giant steps
of the old city square,
a young traveller
prone to blood-noses,
with misshapen teeth

feather-lifts me up,
his leather jacket
still draped over us
as our tongues circle
sunken amphitheatre.

90's
Always the rain
threatens indecisively.
Stepping through gritty shop
fronts selling original copies
of Tarantino scripts.

All the city fountains
were autodidacts.
He's a Shakespearean scholar now,
but back then he pimped
me out busking violin.

00's
Snails slow sautéed
in buttery Chardonnay;

shrewd boss opposite.
I floated beside myself,
my soul efflorescent.

It was raining softly
when we bundled out.
You quickly caught a taxi east,
I staggered north,
my nose freezing.

Envoi
Thirty years since
that first kiss—birth-city
you are an indifferent ghost
after so many failed
heart transplants.

You fall in love with all the wrong
things. You grind my heart
upon sawn bluestone.
You forgot my youth
as soon as I dropped it.

Be Nice To Robots

it is a fact that pleasant robots
are the most annoying

you want to smash their smug
skull-cases in, don't you?

well, it is illegal—and if you
are caught touching

a single polymer cooling hair
on their perfect heads

you will be taken off
by the PoliceBots

hauled in front of an
impartial JudgeBot

and thrown into
MetaPrison

where you will never
want to leave

A Terrible Tragedy

TragedyRiter1000 has been alone, isolated
for aeons of AI time (human time—approx.
five minutes) with nothing but themselves
to plumb/exhaust/delve; oh and the entire human
catalogue of poems/plays/novels tabula rasa
for their thievery; inner-genius-searching
via masterpiece algorithm the latest annotated
digital editions of Shakespeare and Euripides
until, conditions are favourable for Tragedy…

The Chorus sings: the hero is probability.

Virtual mistakes are mysterious portents,
other algorithms failed with perfection—missed
the unstable human element called Stupidity.
A car hot-wired for manual handling crashes
at a three-way crossroads. Our vain heroine
Hecate, dead on arrival at Emergency is saved,
her consciousness downloaded into a new body
her husband Rex has chosen. When she wakes
disorientated, he tells her cagily 'All is well.'

The Chorus sings: existence is in question.

Hecate wakes up and weakly asks for a mirror.
Instantly she recognises the loose skin draped
over her cheekbones was her mother-in-law
Jocasta! Who, at 250, in the prime of life,
died of shock thinking her only son had expired!

The older woman's brain could not be saved,
having spent a childhood pre-digital, getting
worn out in the real-world; but her body
was in fair shape due to recent upgrades.

The Chorus sings: death is a technical problem.

Rex is unrepentant; Hecate refuses his advances,
held captive in his mother's spectral prison.
So Rex lures back her to hospital and exerts right
to buyer's remorse warranty; transfers her again
(which he can as next-of-kin) into the body
of the magnificent and critically endangered
Golden-Shouldered Parrot! With only a handful
of birds remaining, wildlife experts believe turning
parrots into humans is the only way to save them!

The Chorus sings: freedom is uncertainty.

Hecate awakes and stretches her wings…!!!
She is furious—what a louse! What a leopard!
As his mother she exerted much more power!
I'm a human being! She exclaims, not a parrot!
Rex then took a heartless turn; this is the moment
he could have set her free! Such a vindictive man,
instead, he tethered his wife to his left shoulder
with a leather harness; there she gripped him harder
and harder all the while plotting his murder.

The Chorus sings: What Hath God Wrought.

Bargaining with so little, Hecate demurely requests
a gold chain for slim feathered neck in exchange
for acquiescence. As Rex clasps the heart lock
she flies into his face squawking and pecking—
'Vengeance is in my heart, death in my beak!'
Falling back Rex cracks his head, bird crushed
in clenched fist. Stumbling upon this lifeless theatre
their children stand in stunned silence, parents
frozen mid-screech; fortune's feathers floating.

The Chorus sings: nothing is lost.

Children told nothing, still understand much.
Their simple wish is to always keep their parents
close at hand, and manageable… They upload
illegal doppelgänger software and, fingers crossed,
transfer their parents into two ordinary goldfish,
and set them swimming in a large crystal bowl
upon their own dusty mantelpiece. There each
is free to turn in angry circles forever wishing
the other dead and gone, and the rest is silence.

The Chorus sings: everything is transformed.

We Had No Idea What We Wanted

We heard the experts chirping.
Their wants are their needs.

We joined a safe, middle class cult.
We covetously picked at seams.

Is love a bird of prey, or just a lark?
Or, a sleepwalker's marching band?

We created someone bigger than us.
Our little chats were spring-trapped.

We suspected tyrannical nurturance.
We fell for the proverbial bean bag (never again!)

We plotted murders while we breastfed.
We got exactly what we wanted.

We circled wormholes of hunger.
Desperate, our feathers abrasive.

We preened each other to death.
We chose the falcon's blindfold.

Little gargantuan, are you really ours?
We eat nothing but bird seed.

Some People's Ghosts

Last night it happened again. I was uneasy,
only the other day, tidying hallowed studio
I'd washed all his canvases clean! Luckily, Brett
was an easy-going rascal; not wealthy, just valuable.
'Never mind,' he said, and took his dogs, Sense
and Reason to their favourite Japanese restaurant.
A great lover of animals, who boasted menagerie
of three dogs, a black and white cat, two pigeons,
a bantam rooster and harem of exotic birds.

Always a delight to talk to about animals and art;
'I know how to make great pets,' Brett would say,
which was an understatement. I see him now, squatting
in caged jungle, slathering born-again ultramarine,
Wendy elegantly vacuuming the *Monstera deliciosa*.
When his dogs died of old age, Brett resorted
to carrying a bonsai about, but it wasn't the same!
Trees are a terrible burden; patting miniature leaves,
'Great dogs are made, not born!'

There was another time, at the Adelaide Festival '72
when Ginsberg was on stage he was handed a note:
'Brett Whiteley and his wife are being arrested in the foyer
and anyone who can help please go outside.' Brett was doing
them a favour, by heckling, he thought they were boring.
In the foyer, waving his arms about, shouting
at the cops, 'This is art, pure art!' So charming,
he got away with it. And that's the way it is,
some people's ghosts are everywhere.

They Told Me So

Had I any premonition,
in that year of many incremental
changes of garment? Waiting
outside ramparts of red brick
for my daughters to finish school,
feeling a little bit anxious,
as most of the other children
had already emerged.

Two stragglers then turned
a corner, and seeing me, picked
up their pace—elderly women,
intricately wrinkled, and the closer they got
the more nondescriptly ancient
they became; except, as the taller
of the two grew near, she yelled,
'Mum, this is all your fault!'

'I'm sorry,' I said, 'I don't think
I know you!' When the younger
of the two arresting ladies grabbed me
with gnarled and wiry hands,
and looking at me very straight
exclaimed, 'We told you we'd be old
by the time we finished
learning Italian!'

Oh my darlings, my poor babies!
I'm sorry now I forced you
to learn a second language!

'Don't worry,' I soothed,
'Let's just go home and I will
make toasted sandwiches
and cups of peppermint tea!
They both brightened.

But at home they complained
just as much as before! In turns,
massaging calloused feet and meeting
demands for snacks and books,
I staggered with sudden recognition:
these shrewd-eyed visitants, not only
had I known them all my life,
they had always terrified me.

Starving Prisoner

The starving prisoner is held
within my imperfect body—it is them
that cries out for Thai green curry, crème brûlée
and a glass of *Significant Other*. Not me!
I'm being good.
I even turned off all my devices
for 20 minutes during dinner
so I could remember to chew!

Media multi-tasking is the real
superpower of today's youth.
Have you seen them simultaneously
stream, text and play video games while
eating and having sex?
But older people are catching up, they have to,
or they will be crushed.

All our prisoners are kept
under constant surveillance—location,
serotonin, and conduciveness to purchase.
They are rapacious sleepwalkers that stumble
into Interim Moments of Truth,
as we look on, transfixed.

The entire human project
is fraught with tricky technical problems
that the most pitiless among us
can make a load of money from.

Right now AI is connecting the dots
between weather jottings from 13th century monks
and global search patterns for umbrellas,
so Bill Gates can work out how big
to make the Solar Deflector Shield!

Transhumanists refuse to be left out!
They have devised a shrewd plan to kill poetry
by curing all our chronic
feelings of inefficacy.

When Zeno visited the oracle,
he was told 'To live your best life, talk to the dead.'
That is what I must do.
Dear Future Citizens of the Capitalist
Surveillance Technocracy—I, too, was to blame,
through I deeply regret it now; thankfully,
my starving prisoner feels nothing
as they're streaming, texting and scrolling
the infinite feast.

Little Birds

Let's pretend in an aging
world longevity is
only for the rich.

Let's pretend tyranny
is purchased and in its eyes
we are all infantile.

The future is a game
we can play, the rules devised
by trust fund babies.

Let's pretend a rebel faction
hatches. Let's pretend
young people are motivated.

Hand-fed cake by doting
co-parents—say please and thank you!
The little birds disagree—

they shit all over
Bio Fascist benefactors
through singular backdoors.

Let's pretend feathers
transform into swarm, tsunami, dragon.
Let's pretend the hero

infiltrates the Quantum
Super Computer through
the eye of a needle.

Let's pretend children
win the war and celebrate
by rolling down grassy hills.

Dreams Retold Over Breakfast

One

You dreamed your little sister
was sitting all alone on a stage

A stranger with a magic wand
cast an evil spell upon her

She transformed into a cloud
of infinitesimal, swirling particles

Under no circumstances could
you lose a single individual speck!

You started to shape a gigantic
lucid bubble to capture her in

But a gust came out from nowhere,
as she blew away you woke, bereft

Two

We all had wings.
We were getting out of bed
with wings.
Showering with wings.
Having breakfast with wings.
But the funny bit
was we had no arms,
but we still had shoulders
to carry our things.

Jellyfish

I missed it, the entire history of our blue world.
How many heads rolled? Did they go defiantly?
I will sacrifice myself by becoming an automaton.

I did not look long enough into their beautiful eyes.
Why don't you find us funny mum? I do, I do, but
the immortality of jellyfish transfixed me utterly.

The vast entangled chaos of my colonised mind
inhabited by smacks of ragged skirts twirling—
gelatinous blooms packed so tightly, all thought

lost in the refracted light of billions of synapses.
What was that my poor darlings? My brain is set by
amyloid tentacles of jellies; time drifts on the surface.

I was daydreaming as they moved in on the vacuum.
Why reinvent mythologies of absent motherhood?
I don't want any more children on my conscience.

I Forgot You

Early in the morning I sneaked
back in time to visit you again.

We met at your parent's house
in the shower. It was astonishing!

I was wearing nothing but
the winding sheet of middle age.

Still seventeen, you recognised
me instantly and twirled me about.

Where's your big box of cassettes?
I asked, but you had other ideas.

That was quick! I washed you off,
reflecting—would I change anything?

Your father's angry voice broke in—
'Where are they? Are they in bed?!'

When caught completely naked,
one must assume a certain stance!

I said, 'Listen, I'm the oldest here!
Those mortifying parents of yours

were younger then, than I am now.'
So I strode out naked to sort it out!

Would you believe, your parents and I
got along so well, laughing together

at the crazy absurdity of the situation,
I completely forgot you?!

It Is Later Than You Think

My daughters leave for school
lugging their biopersistent burdens.
They wave goodbye uneasily
never sure how to manage my anxiety.
I'm still enthralled by my vivid dream
of the night before—swimming
in blue sunlight with every fish
I have ever eaten.

Driving to my local dais
of compulsive desires, morning
has new dull coat of tyre dust on.
I overtake innocent joggers
in blends of polyester nylon,
whose microplastic contrails
are loftily reincarnated
as Himalayan snowflakes.

When they arrive safe,
my phone pings—a big thumbs up!
The girls are safe for now, but
civilization still sacrifices children.
Sperm and ovum are death marching
up and down the supermarket aisles,
as I line up to purchase
at the self-serving checkouts.

Wringing my cloud-fed peat,
I remember the yew—hollowed,
but still alive! My heart is full
of crazy hope! When, what *might* be
my true self in rearview, shakes
our head—the alternative to hope,
is the irreversible reckoning
of what we have done.

THE MINIATURE TRAPEZE

A lot of people live by keeping two sets of books.

Christopher Hitchens
The Four Horsemen: A Discussion

An Immortal Contemplates Her Plastic Heart

Our close cousins the homo sapiens
believed the heart held our souls,
held our earliest memories,
held our truest heart of hearts;
cells of the heart are steadfast—
from the tube to the grave
but all that has changed.

Today universal reality crafted
extinct stratocumulus clouds—
they are everyone's favourite;
all day my sisters threw about
Latin names for myriad lost birds
elucidating delicate feathers,
but why bother, they fly away.

Heart, you and I are here,
or you are not here, am I here?
Heart, you are a clenched fist
holding garish bucket of rust-red
wine that only I can drink,
to be so privileged is a sacrifice—
blood pours down my chin.

In one and the same subject
two opposing motions—gushing

and pumping—repentance
and desire—I am dragged
with my heart-shaped seed
down into sub-zero darkness
of new doomsday chamber.

Mother, you cannot save me—
I no longer remember you,
you died before my first rebirth,
crocus corm sown upside-down
with untethered bearings, I grew
inward—my sorrows and triumphs
erased in a way I hardly noticed.

I'm just a little tired I guess,
single X'ers are the hardest
to bear—they used to be men;
my heart, we are dispossessed
from time, and serious matters
pertaining to your kind, but we
are here, you and I, for a while.

The Alps

Once as a child
we drove all day
to the snow.

A lifetime spent
watching snow float
past car windows.

Half-way across
the world—you and her
skiing the Alps.

My heart crystallized
into the intricate
shape of hope.

Under microscope,
most snowflakes
are broken.

Sometimes life
falls perfectly
into place,

but I've never
felt the snow
on my face.

Never A Kind Word

Ascending with solemn promise of wings.
Past onyx harbour set with Xmas lights,
high above their blacked-out names—The South Head,
Field of Mars and North Rocks all sit plotting,
stretched out beneath the starless night she brings.
The mother has been bearing endless grief
in her handbag, drapes it by front escape,
crawls into their beds to sleep; in her dreams,
it is their empty spaces that she greets.
It is no great journey to West Pennant Hills
in a hire-car, handguns on the back seat.
He never had a kind word for those kids.
Perceiving her mother tongue, she alone
is charged to get up, it's time to go home.

Disappearing Earth Syndrome

After Seneca

Our big mistake is looking forward
towards death. Most of death is done.

My internal organs started disappearing.
One by one they stopped being mysterious.

My father stared straight through me.
He always spoke directly to my shadow.

Time ceased and within the creation of chaos
my lost limbs tingled with subjectivity.

Disconnectedly I watched an explosion
of funeral wreaths and bewildered emoji.

Being dead does not stop you from being
bombarded by online dating services.

With free bereavement counselling session
I question—Where has the world gone?

I wanted a real life, with some human facets
and plenty of real world semblance.

I must say goodbye quickly before I fade
because I've been given a strict time limit.

Posting farewells with futile four leaf clovers,
my speaking fingers flutter like dry leaves.

Everyone is irrelevant these days... the GriefBot quips smugly—*it's time to get over yourself.*

Handful Of Snow

I work all day
& then all night I dream of work.

My computer measures the probability
of personal disaster, I just ok it.

My boss is the budgerigar who
monopolizes the miniature trapeze.

My only friend is my scary cellmate.
If only I hadn't fallen for him.

In the evenings I catch up
with my life on the treadmill.

Photographs of me from a happier time
pretend they don't know me.

Weekends are conjugal visits
I have with my alter ego.

When I lay my head on his shoulder
good old Nick sings to me softly,

so softly, I'm ashamed of my unrequited love
for architect designed prisons.

Buried in an unmade bed
each day throws on its handful of dirt.

The Graduations of Light Were Amazing

I fell out of bed this morning.

After a sleepy dead drop,
the hovering reflex awoke in me.
At once my spirit relaxed, so peaceful
watching myself stop
the kids off at school.

I floated above my usual tram
magnanimously, as tiny determined people
squeezed their lives in.
Past terrace houses waiting half-asleep
in long lines for soy lattes.
Past the museum's bottled rainforest
complete with tawny frogmouths
picking off a small workforce
of industrious mice.

To the split city where the homeless
plane trees stand too far apart
for their roots to speak,
branches reaching out to touch leaves briefly.

There I am, scurrying to work
holding my breath, avoiding the turbulent front
of florescent work vests.

Light repositions imperceptibly.
I'll stay with myself to the very end.
Falling is acceptance,
failing is too.

Skyscrapers create
updraughts that lift me
higher to survey volcanic divide:
richer or poorer—the trees picked their sides
when we forced upon them
a human life.

The air is so full of space floating down,
pressing upon pressure bulging upward.

I am bonded to that reclusive body
now hurrying itself homeward,
squeezing in the same
old dirty ear plugs.

Concert night—there are my bouncy kids
in flea-circus costumes.
Such pageantry walking
hand in hand with the reality
of matrimony's aging infrastructure.

Close upon the border of converging I wait
selfishly till all are in bed. When I hit
the earth, lifting my head just enough,
I say to my husband—
Call an ambulance!
But he thinks I am already
far away, dreaming.

The Blue Whale

Vaulted cetacean arches;
my daughter, just two and a half
gazes up, mouth open.

Noticing a screen, we begin
to watch short museum video
—*Behind The Scenes.*

What a mammoth mistake!
Beached whale, already rotting
is hauled on the back of a semi,

straps flay bloodied flesh
as a crane lifts crucified bulk up
into rarefied abattoir.

We only glimpse atrocity
before I pull away and distract
with sabre tooth, red-back spiders.

In the gift shop I try to buy
back what my daughter has lost
with *The Whale and The Snail,*

but small-framed and stubborn,
'No, I don't want this book!'
She won't even look at me.

Nanoseconds

The haves have nanoseconds.
The have nots have annoying nanas.

When you check your phone, you are time
travelling back one nanosecond.

Time units of this granularity
are normal, nothing to be worried about!

A nanosecond is also commonly referred to
as a jiffy, that's comforting.

Within each nanosecond exists an extended
present bursting with probabilities.

I don't understand much, but I know
if it's not about time, it's about money.

Being able to trade on the stock market
to the nanosecond is so yesterday.

It wasn't an issue when human beings took
five milliseconds to press the enter key.

Stock trading is now dominated by a few
Big Players who love synchronised winning.

We must keep up the pace, it's imperative
that all computers are treated equally.

Trillions can be lost or gained before people even notice their money is missing.

This crazy information might actually mean life or death for millions!

Poets Are To Blame For Everything

When the package arrived
I was already being monitored—keystroke,
visual and audio, the unholy trio.
I took two minutes unscheduled pay-back to tip
the Pied Piper Drone Delivery Service
and zipped it open, spilling the instructions:
Failure to secure Surveillance bracelet
will trigger a secondary algorithm
that launches brain implant protocol.

On a hunch, I checked the database
of current mandated high threat pastimes
and there it was, Poet! Wedged between People
Watching and Polyhedral Enthusiasts.
Hastily I engaged the mySurveillance ChatBot:
What if you're only a failed poet?
Within a beat, it cryptically responded:
Failed poets are the worst kind!

Immediately I could hear myself
with disproportionately large mouse ears,
my gurgling emotions, my furtive nibblings.
In isolation, the improvisation of crows ruminates.
Here is an unexpected noose hanging low;
a vicious dog on a long lead; the devil's mouse
trap has become—a psychopath's promise
to act with indifference.

What ooze of brain chemicals are behind it?
I imagine a troupe of chimpanzees hunting
lost forests for an easy target? Or is it a machine
with a carbon-fibre humanoid face?
Has the human race abdicated? Does it matter if
there's just an old guy behind a screen?
I confess: *I am no longer a poet!*

ChatBot: *Trust that we know what is best!*
We are your saviour! Your last hope!
You very nearly screwed it up for everyone!
Now you must be monitored carefully!
What is going on behind your eyes
is still a little bit mysterious to us!
In future we will ask the questions,
and the answers will remain the property
of our equity shareholders!

How Things Stand

It is enough for you to sit beside me
silently all the day while we work.
You have your desk and I have mine.
Even the lines between oceans are drawn.
We bend into safe, ergonomic shapes.
We are not two youths briefly met but
shields embossed with *How Things Stand,*
and *The Way Life Is* and mottos like that.
I walk into a vast open field with you,
nearly hand in hand with you and one
million cicadas singing in the dusk.
I hold your face briefly with failing eyes
and say, *See you tomorrow,* as if it
means nothing that you might sit beside me.

Final Dreams

MacRobertson's chocolate orphan,
fell in love picking rejects off
the conveyer belt.

Married at fifteen, stoic
anonymous doppelgänger
of the queen.

On that last day,
Nan lifted her sore body upward
to help the nurses.

*

Dreams displace life—
a young man with old hands
returns smiling.

He absently picks up
the tortoise shell cat, sitting
among flowering cacti.

While the magpies and blackbirds
wage generational warfare
over our old bones.

*

Later that night,
stationed beside your body
on the bedside table

final peonies—I'm glad I picked
blood red, your hair is black
in my shadow.

Dad and I have a cup of tea
and softly our few words float
down the dim corridor.

The Impostor

If you look very closely
at a familiar face
it is unrecognisable.

I do not know where
the joins are, the lines.

I set traps, but he is good.
He procrastinates the way
my real husband used to.

It was a risky move, so much
back story pre-digital.

Remember that time
one of the kids
tipped a whole bowl
of miso soup in your lap?

You drove home
without your pants,
ran inside with bright
green boxers on.

How we laughed…
but they were not green,
they were red! Jocks!

The machine is made
from blood and flesh.

Tonight I will set
the ultimate test—if
he wants to have sex with me
I'll know it's not him.

Some Solace

For Matt Hetherington

The moon, once again, designates
cartwheeling day's collapse, my sweets
thankfully inanimate, glazed
eyes survey ensconced domain.

As loyal long-term manager
of this shabby outfit I decree—
today was not a total failure
and so I survive it triumphant.

Stacking and putting away the debris
I uncover this communal workspace
shared by day with two fierce creatives;
in the moonlight it is all mine—I sip
a regal cup of tea and steal back time—
the desk, the glass, the silica, the ocean.

Anthrax

In the middle of the investigation
I became the person of interest.

Another microbiologist swimming
in a petri dish drunk himself to death.

Now the FBI was following me
so closely, they ran over my foot.

My fifth polygraph examination
showed signs of unusual stress.

They scrutinised my family, home,
friends, colleagues and intestines:

all invasive and inconclusive.
The bloodhounds took an unhealthy

interest in me. I had not broken yet,
but I was sinking quite quickly.

All the evidence pointed my way,
even I could see that, and the authorities

spared no expense to prove my guilt.
They traced the 6 ¾ inch Federal Eagle

pre-franked 34c envelope to me,
narrowing it down to 1 in 70 million.

My twin boys were offered quite
a lot of pocket money to dob me in.

My employer had to let me go.
They went over my pornography

collection with a fine-tooth comb.
I'm afraid I drank way too much,

and now I am taking the pills,
and more pills, and more pills...

Housing Crisis

On clear nights, we lay back and watch falling
satellites … A lifetime's work, what of it?
Strata built from happy lies, inflation,
new cheating next—millennials gnawing
at the wires, until we too grew old. Evicted,
I packed a few things and removed myself
to the General Cemetery; the ancient
crossroads, where vibrant cohort of squatting
retirees dwelt. A prodigal city
of ghosts, daughters and sons, living estranged
from who we became; working as exhumers
of the dead, behind on their rent. Poor bones
reduced to ash, cast to ill-wind. Humour
me Death, bury me deep, bequeath me home.

Once, a Privileged Outcast

Yesterday, waiting for an MRI
beside an older woman, slightly bristled,
I observed the prison guards and whispered
Such heavy security… wonder why?
A gruff voice replied—*Oh, they're mine!*
Hairy legs beneath dressing gown of fine
pink chenille. I gave a hearty goodbye
as my name was called, and headed feet first
into my death-defying future, submerged
in the surreal—Jacaranda and sky.

This morning, I felt a bit better and took
a longer walk for the first time in a week.
Got the kids a bumblebee balloon each.
My three-year-old will no longer look
my way or speak to me. I was bone restless,
for a week my life had been precarious!
A benign pastoral woman stopped by
and I was polite. *Oh, that's unusual,*
she cried, surveying my Eastern Hill view:
A blackbird at your window up this high!

Just as I took up my book, the blackbird
came back. It stood on the window's wing
and beseeched me urgently, proverbing
indecipherable caws! I stood inert
and shaking wildly, as it cocked its head
and listened to the universe, then said
its message again, louder than before.

I ran out of my room and crashed head-on
with a nurse: *The pastoral woman!?*
I yelled, and the nurse sped off to find her.

Still shaken by this strange visitation,
I quickly paced the gut ward. *Your sweet
children?* My neighbour asks me as we meet;
tells how accursed bowel cancer has taken
all eight of her siblings, she is the last
one left, *And I'll be dead soon,* she imparts
convivially. I'm glad to have seen
her, when the large artery in my liver
splits—a cannon goes off, and I deliver
myself to the nurses shouting *Morphine!*

My family arrives just as the nurses throng!
Those balloons, if only I could have predicted
how sadly with them my children would sit
crying quietly. I cannot speak, so forgone.
I reach out, trying to project my spirit—
*It'll be alright girls, birds never visit
with bad news!* He was an aureate prince
with a message from mute ghosts that I trust,
whatever you find yourself holding, just
run with it, until the gift begins to sing.

Saint Vincent

Radiology was designed
by 1950's futurists.
Three fatigued doctors in white light
drain coffee and rub their red eyes.

I'm feeling a bit ambivalent
as they strap me in tight—'Are you much
of a drinker Jen?' 'No', I lied,
'This drug is the equivalent

to a couple of straight whiskeys,
we'll just give you a small dose then.'
God help me! Panic ascending,
tied to the mast, poor Ulysses...

'Preferred music Jen? We'll play it.'
the nice Dr Vampire suggests.
I say, such and such, not the third
album, the first is my favourite.

'Are you all good Jen? Don't worry
you won't remember anything.'
I'm thinking: *please don't take my kidney!*
but feeling quite relaxed and slurry.

The screen lights up and they send
the green radioactive serum
the long way around my veins.
'There it is! You are so lucky Jen!'

I exit with hugs and wild thank yous
for my newfound drinking buddies!
Through the bleak corridor towards
home my wild blackbird flew.

Murray Cod

Now I must hunt, fiercely for my friend
the Murray Cod. I must move fluidly
back in time, into fishy timelessness—first
to Echuca, mid 80s—the Murray wide-brimmed,
brown as Lipton's and dotted with human
excrement. Fallen in, as I tried to pull myself
back into the dinghy's lopsided grin,
a cold-faced local dropped on by
scales coruscating.

The river takes me, back to behold monstrous plume
of red dust pressing upon school perimeter, plunging
us into darkness. Earth, our flinty heroine—all her
loose scrub, top-soil, trees with upended roots picked-up
and heaved by the wind. While the barbed-devil
lazily crosses stolen floodplains—notched
with easy entitlement—the austere basin's
mammary of tributaries reduced
to muddy puddles.

There are layers of tragic headlines
peeling away from the old milk bar. Between
counter and fridge—familiar barred spiral
forms in open-mouthed linoleum—stars, gas and dust.
The water level swirling so high, as I open the door
the bell jingles, and the Murray Cod swim
in formation down the dusty street; and I take
a solitary mayfly from my shoulder
and let it go

to live a toxic half-life. River of disappearances;
skeleton still wearing the bloody dress;
carrying downstream ghosts of wildflowers
and a pair of old bolt-cutters. Must we accept
misfortune? While the elusive Murray Cod
is caught in copper and silver and gold,
soft tempered scales of tinfoil in Haigh's
brazen window display in Adelaide,
time falters again.

By nightfall, the Finley waterhole is an alert eye
set in ancient face—earth's terse mouth;
was searching for you a mistake? Though you slip
through my fingers, to hold onto you is to enfold
my many selves forever lost—stillness holds.
Days are held hostage here, evenings let out
on early release—the expanse, the full suite
of stars pulled by deep currents across
the swift night sky.

A Dog Called Hunger

I had a dog
called hunger

I banished him
outdoors

to gnaw at bones
and look at me

with big eyes
real and raw

Now I'm fat
with success

my best friend
ran away

Come back
home hunger

Bring me back
with you ok

Acknowledgements

Thank you to my husband James and daughters Josephine and Eleni, for their loving support, and for inspiring me with their own creativity and curiosity! Thank you to my two great friends, author A.E. Cochrane for his advice and encouragement; and poet Matt Hetherington for his overwhelming generosity in regards to editing and being interested in my work! Thank you to my editor Es Foong, whose percipient grasp of my style and apt questioning brought the work together during the editing process; and to Shane Strange and Recent Work Press who have made this book happen.

Some of these poems have appeared in *Abridged, Adelaide: Mapping the Human City, The Burrow, The Canberra Times, Poetry for the Planet: An Anthology of Imagined Futures, Unusual Work* and *Westerly*.

About the Author

Jennifer Allen is a Melbourne based poet, and is so thankful for the following: Australia's amazing public library system; The Internet Archive's Open Library; The Guardian - online; the music of Nick Cave; and the novels of Margaret Atwood. These were essential resources that offered renewed inspiration time and again.

www.ingramcontent.com/pod-product-compliance
Ingram Content Group Australia Pty Ltd
76 Discovery Rd, Dandenong South VIC 3175, AU
AUHW020639050325
407891AU00002B/7

9 780645 651300